AFTER ENCHANTMENT

POEMS BY
SUSAN KAY SCHEID

ORIGINAL WATERCOLORS
BY
ELIZABETH SCHEID

ISBN: 1478316101
ISBN 13: 9781478316107
Library of Congress Control Number: 2012913788

North Charleston, South Carolina

Cover Images courtesy of author
Acknowledgements
    Tidal Basin Review: "Outside In"
    Requiem Magazine: "Elegy for RCG," "Speaking of Death"
    Rose Red Review: "Prince Charming," "Snow White's Math Problem"

For Chris, Alex and Sam.

*For George Scheid who started me on this journey
by way of a childhood filled with poems,
fairy tales, and corny jokes.*

TABLE OF CONTENTS

The Quest

~ I want to go out into the world
of marvels and adventures

(Steinbeck, *The Acts of King Arthur and His Noble Knights*)

PRINCE CHARMING

He was a Buddhist,
riding his meditation,
the horse's hooves his mantra.
He breathed in rhythm with the trees.

The princess was an illusion.
The kiss a metaphor
for what he did not know.

And he, like others before him,
knew that where the story ends
is actually its beginning.

THE IMPORTANCE OF WORDS

Buddha once said, *Be*
in this world,
but not
of it.

Thus, I carry
a preposition
in my pocket
in case I meet
an obstacle—
instead of going *around*
I can go *through*.

DRINKING COFFEE WITH JESUS

I was surprised to learn he likes both cream and sugar,
figuring he would drink it black, unadulterated.

We began with talk of the weather, social niceties.
I tried not to sound demanding or ungrateful
about the lack of winter or the early spring
that caused my daffodils to bloom in February
or even about the infestation of ants, who awakened
when the earth began to warm and found the sugar
in my kitchen sweeter than any nectar in the yard.

He was unassuming and small, thin,
almost frail looking in a faded plaid shirt
and jeans, clean shaven. He looked so young.
He listened to me talk about nothing,
nodding his head, and stirring his coffee,
the soft ring of his spoon as it grazed
the rim on his flowered cup, like tiny bells
chiming in the distance.
He even seemed interested.

No one bothered us in the back of the coffee shop.
No one came by to lobby favors or miracles.
They left us to our quiet conversation
two old friends catching up on life
sitting in the late afternoon sun,
golden pink in its light,
ephemeral in its promise.

Sleeping Beauty

Every night the prince calls out to me
to return to bed and his dreams.

Insomnia is my friend now.
I have no use for sleep these days.

For those who criticize, I say
let me wander with Death
atop the walls of the night,
for only in that darkness
do I truly feel awake.

SPEAKING OF DEATH
A LETTER TO THE GRIM REAPER

Dear Grim Reaper,

When it comes near my time, would you be so kind
as to let me know in advance? I swear
I will not tell a soul. Our secret will be safe.

I would like to be able to prepare, go with elegance,
as if we were off to the opera one last time,
dressed to the nines. I'll wear my long gloves
and you can wear your top hat and cape,
carry me on your arm like a lady.
We can leave when the fat lady sings, or
maybe a little before.

Don't worry. I know that like Cinderella,
the gown is rented, the clock will chime
one final note for me and then it's all mice
and pumpkins, but let me enjoy the journey.

While I am asking, can we have music and laughter?
I don't want to feel like some small animal
trapped by its own death, the taste of fear
and blood the last thing it remembers, before –
well, I think you know what I mean.

Please send me your engraved invitation or
leave your off-white calling card by the door.
I will look for it, but not too soon.

Thank you for your consideration.

I remain cordially yours,

Before

When asked what she did before
she had children.
She answered:
I walked the world with closed eyes.

Vision

A door closes.
A window opens.
People shout
Jump, jump.

It takes a far-sighted person
to see the encroaching darkness
is not a void, but a pair of wings
with which to fly.

Buddha

Buddha said
Un-attach.
When suffering comes
touch the earth
connect
to the root of all roots.
And when suffering finds you
be not the archer
nor the arrow.
Be the air
which parts
and re-unites.
Only air understands
this movement
and forgives.

The Villain

*~ She raised her black eyes and saw her lovely
sister queens licking their lips like wolves
about a bleeding slaughter*

(Steinbeck, *The Acts of King Arthur and His Noble Knights*)

THE WICKED WITCH REACHES STEPS 8 AND 9
(WHEREIN SHE MUST APOLOGIZE AND MAKE AMENDS TO THOSE SHE HAS HARMED)

Dear All,

I hate to write a group letter; however,
I don't want to overlook any transgressions.

I have reached a point in my rehabilitation
where I have acceded to my Higher Power and
I am ready to make amends.

To those whom I have caused physical or
emotional harm, I am sorry.

To the frogs, snakes and other creatures, I realize
what an insult it has been cursing humans
with your life form.
I am sorry.

To children, dogs, and small magical beings,
I should never have threatened or terrorized you,
with either my size or power.
I am sorry.

To stepmothers, crows, old women,
people with warts, my actions have given you
a bad reputation.
I am sorry.

As a positive step, I have divested myself of flying monkeys.
I am now a vegetarian and no longer drink
potions. I avoid sweets. I grow my own vegetables.

I hired an image consultant, had my colors done.
I gave up the color black. Turns out, I'm a Spring.

I am taking voice lessons.
I am writing poetry instead of incantations.
I have gone to counseling for my self-esteem.

I can only hope that from this day forward you can forgive me
and we can live happily ever after.

Best regards,
WW

THE GREAT DEBATE

Katie did.
Katie didn't.
Katie did.

The argument went on and on
night after night.
All summer.
Every evening began
a new round in the debate.

Katie did.
Katie didn't.
Katie did.

We lay in our beds
light still holding onto the sky
dark silhouette of pines
looming outside the windows.

Katie didn't.

Sometimes there was a pause
as if new evidence in Katie's case
had come to light for review
all sides taking it into consideration.

Katie did.
Katie didn't.
The disagreement continued.

It continued as the sky relaxed
and fell into darkness,
became louder as Big Bear appeared,
took his position on the matter.

Katie did.
As the archer raised his bow
concurring with the crowd.

Katie didn't.
As we tried to stay awake long enough
to hear the outcome of her fate,
eyes weighted by the rocking rhythm.

Katie did.
Katie didn't.

Meanwhile, we surrendered to nocturnal journeys
far from Katie and her advocates.

Our reveries were interrupted only
by the creep of morning and the doves
asking "Who-hoo, who? Who? Who?"
No one ever answered them,
but we always knew in our hearts
that it was never Katie.

GOSSIP

You may close the mouth of an oven,
but how do you close the mouth of a town?
        ~Indian proverb

He said what she thought
and what everyone had heard.
One voice repeated
only every other word.

Truth looked a little frayed
as mouths chewed holes
like hungry moths
in its delicate fabric,
allowing a space
for vipers to nest.

DEPOSITION OF RUMPLESTILTSKIN

1. My name is Rumplestiltskin.
   I am an Enchanted Being.
   My occupation is spinning straw into gold,
   but I also garden, play banjo and raise chickens.

2. I deny perpetrating fraud.
   It was the girl's father who boasted
   of her skills. I actually do know
   how to spin.

3. I am not a kidnapper.
   It was never about the baby.
   I felt sorry for her, but I needed collateral up front –
   you're a businessman, you understand that.

4. I gave her every opportunity to guess my name.
   Off the record, I had secretly hoped
   she would escape. By that I mean
   take the baby and run far away.

5. I would have told her to marry for love.
   No one can spin that.

Outside In

. . . in trying to heal the wound that never heals,
lies the strangeness, the inventiveness of a man's work
(Garcia Lorca)

1. Outside

I know about the strip searches after our visits
as if our presence left you with a piece of humanity
that had to be removed.

I know how you kept to yourself, reading
praying, adrift in darkness,
to avoid answering dangerous questions.

I know you were embarrassed by the number of letters
arriving daily, missives from those who loved and missed you,
while others around you were often ignored.

I know on the nights you could not phone, how you asked
God to send a message that you were safe
so we would sleep quietly, dreamlessly.

I know you saved apples and crackers, stockpiled
them like treasures, to improvise pie and a slice
of home on a Sunday afternoon.

I know how you learned that trust
could be a word divided
between tru(e) and us.

2. Inside

On the day you returned, we stood outside in the sleety rain,
nothing but a cartoon umbrella to protect us,
and we waited for the gates to open.

We watched you approach in too-big clothes
carrying the remnants of your life
in a transparent bag.

There were no secrets that day.

And after you had showered,
regained your human scent,
we fed you a king's banquet
grilled cheese and tomato soup.
We covered nearly every inch of you
our skin on your skin
as if to hold you in that moment forever.

And on that first night, you found the sky unbearable,
all that open space and vulnerability.

And that was how I came to know the prison
you carried home from your cinderblock lodging.

The one you hide behind your smile
the one under your easygoing laugh
the one residing in the dark spot of your eyes.

I know this prison rattles its chains inside you;
my ear pressed to your chest, I think I hear
the metallic sound of keys, the click of a lock.

I am not sure whether it is opening or closing,
I only know that I am on the outside
and I am trying to get in.

B. B. Wolf

I know you want me to be black.
I am gray.
A mixture between dark and light.
It's where I live, like the forest itself,
sunlight and shadow cohabitating.
Sometimes though you have to watch your step.

It can be difficult to live in a world
always hungry for a villain,
instinct versus intelligence.
My money is on instinct.

While I may or may not have threatened some pigs,
chased a basket of goodies along a path,
I never broke any laws.
Consider my actions food shopping
like the old ladies at market.

My name is whispered late at night,
come take a walk and hear it,
if you're not afraid of the dark.

PREVARICATION

He looked me in the eye
then he lied to me
his lips never sneered
eyes never flashed.
But he lied.

Then I could see it –
the lie – just beneath
his skin, moving around,
as if it were some parasite
burrowing, becoming part of him.

And when he smiled
it almost disappeared.
When I said *I love you*
all I could hear was the lie,
chewing away inside him,
burrowing deeper.

When We Ruled the World

There we stood, dressed like Egyptians
or what we thought Egyptians should look like
from all our *National Geographic* magazines.

Wrapped in old curtains, jewels, tulle,
prancing around like we built the pyramids
while life in our sleepy Ohio town
rolled by on its way to middle America.

Men went to work at the refinery
spewing invisible gas and smoke in the breeze
while women ironed shirts and watched television.

But we did not notice the quiet turning
because we were too busy inventing pictograms,
enslaving younger brothers in our game
of carving scarabs and conquering the desert.

Ancient worlds so enticing because
the glossy pictures were clean –
unlike the paint peeling from too much sulfur,
the houses abandoned when factories closed.

There being no room for Egyptian princes
or pyramids in this Republican county
known for its prized cattle, corn and soybeans.

TINY SHOES

The shoes sit in their corner
and I sit in mine.
We are the watchers.
Sitting and listening for the constant
rhythm of the oxygen, the metronome
of her lungs.

I watch her sleep.
The shoes watch her sleep.
We all watch each other watching
While the metronome counts down
her breaths.

As if all this watching could save her.

The shoes know
and I know
that Death creeps about
in the shadows,
visible in the corner of my eye.

And the metronome counts
and the shoes watch
and I watch
waiting
waiting
waiting for that day
when Death steals her last breath
and shows himself
only as he leaves the room.

The Journey Alone

~ His fingers searched the edges of the door and confirmed that it opened inward, as it must

(Steinbeck, *The Acts of King Arthur and His Noble Knights*)

RAPUNZEL

I've cut my hair.
Keep it short now.
I like the solitude.

I've also modernized the tower.
Installed a dumbwaiter.
It's simpler.

The outside is overwhelming,
all that open space.
I prefer my tower,
where the sun enters my narrow
window in trickles and I get
my reality in small pieces.

Admit it.
Everyone likes a good tower,
the security it provides.
Only some prefer to call it
by another name, like career
or marriage.

The prince once told me,
*You've made your tower
now live in it.*

I do.

DRIVING HOME

There is something about the barn
sitting in solitude amid miles of empty fields
sunlight fills the chinks with corn-colored light
brightening a landscape, where everything
is a different shade of grey.

If hope is the thing with feathers
it is nesting in this barn,
having flown from the small stand
of nearby trees – tall and skinny
huddled like self-conscious teens
around the place where the farmhouse stood.

Cars will come and go on this Ohio road
speed past the broken barn without a second
glance, but the barn will watch and keep
count, as it always has.

And the feathery thing will sing
a deep-throated song
leave its downy feathers
to carpet the barn's
cracked earthen floors.

LITTLE RED

She posted a sign near the edge
of the forest. *Estate Sale*
Everything must go!
Items include: one used hatchet,
one hooded woolen cape
(frayed near the edges),
one picnic basket, furniture,
assorted household items.

Grandmother was gone.
There was nothing
to tie her to the countryside.
So she sold her belongings,
changed her name; moved.

Walking the gray city sidewalks,
black rain coat, leather briefcase in hand,
her ears pricked
smell heightened by the iron scent
of her own blood.
This time when the wolves came,
she would be ready.

Hand Me Down

Every evening my mother pulled her knitting
out of the basket behind her chair.
After the dishes were washed, leftovers shelved,
she sat with her metal needles
counting stitches, colored markers, pattern rows
as if ticking off time.

Like the Fates, she measured and spun.
My life could be counted by stripes
of mittens, hats, sweaters, blankets–
created in her post-prandial meditations.

When she cut her final thread,
put away her last skein of wool
I felt as if my life too had ended.
Until I lifted her needles
took up the frayed yarn
and saw her hands reflected back
as I looked out the dark window.

Cinderella Reflects

Gazing in the mirror,
Cinderella notices the accent of crow's feet,
silvery strands among the gold.
Turning the mirror over,
she braids her hair with a sigh.

She was not happy, one could even say lonely.
No one to talk to in the castle.
Servants (except her own maid)
were considered beneath her and
Charming too busy running his kingdom.

Cinderella glanced about the room.
She had never really fit in here
surrounded by luxuries – jewelry, ball gowns, furs.
Perhaps she had merely substituted
one type of servitude for another.

Then there were the shoes –
colors and fabrics she could hardly imagine,
maybe a few she couldn't.

She had never admitted to anyone,
even her personal maid,
how much she despised shoes,
how even the glass slippers had pinched
made her feel confined.

She preferred to be barefoot.
Feel the earth, the ground on her skin.
The ground never lies to you.

Just like late at night she preferred to sleep
near the fireplace, in solitude,
where her maid would find her
hands and feet dirty from stirring the ashes.

First Light

(for the 33 miners trapped in Chile)

Imagine the first light
bouncing pebbles down the shaft
staining the walls like tears
on grimy coal-washed faces.

The body does not like darkness.
Ask the 33 swallowed in the mouth
of earth's hushed tones.
Devoured but not digested.

Imagine the display of cosmic fireworks
embers burning through strata
trickling into the permanent night
that cradles these men.

Would they delight in this interruption
feel joy to discover a sun which
heretofore had been kept from them?

Would there be relief, like the puncture
of a swollen wound
finally allowed to heal?

Would the fresh air carry in its breeze
the joyous voices from the hilltop?

We can only watch the flags flutter,
brilliant colors in the sun
and wait for the light
to draw them out.

HANSEL AND GRETEL GO TO COLLEGE

She enrolled at a well-known liberal arts school.
Studied ethnology, folklore, myth
learned to decode symbols like wolf,
stepmother, wicked witch.

He chose culinary school.
Moved to the city.
Opened a bakery
specializing in gingerbread.

GOLDILOCKS

She and Baby Bear remained friends for many years.
They corresponded regularly in the warm months,
she in her nearly perfect script
he in his childish scrawl.

She never married,
never found anyone "just right,"
having grown accustomed to the coarseness
of winter fur tinged with the scent
of gristle and bone.

All Hallows Eve

Remember how we loved Halloween
before it was taken from us?
The thrill of walking along
the already-darkened street at supper time.
Leaves reaching down
as if to run
their golden fingers through your golden hair.
It's spooky you would whisper,
your warm breath enlivening me,
as you clasped your hands around my neck,
holding on for dear life.

We wandered with purpose, you and I
under the arches of the trees
amid the other wandering souls
seeking their rest on this night.
Spirits whose gauzy outlines
reflected the night clouds
and the webby branches
on either side of us.

This year, I can no longer
contain my loss.
It tires me.
I will wander alone
still seeking something –
your outline in the trees,

the specter of your hand on my neck,
a warm breath as you whisper
and pass by me.

VISITATION

Every Wednesday at four o'clock
the guards come down to the cold gray lobby
of the Correctional Treatment Facility.
Even the afternoon sun
finds no warmth here.

We watch as they pull out their visitor lists.
Lists with changing names
from one week to the next,
but whose faces remain constant.

Silent faces
screaming to tell their story.

Pained faces
hiding shame.

Questioning faces
trying to understand
a language not their own.

Anxious faces
hoping this is not the week
their loved one has been moved.

Masked faces
full of bravado.

All guarded.

And we are all of these faces
all outsiders waiting,
watching, listening
for guards to call our names.

When all have been stripped
of their pride and their shoes,
when every last belonging has been stowed,
when all have been searched,
down to the tiniest diaper,
the guards take us upstairs.

Upstairs, where our men – boyfriends,
cousins, husbands, brothers –
wait anxiously
one to a table.

All faces brighten in this forty-five minutes
where we can all hold hands, laugh,
smell the clean of children's hair.

The faces of our quarters and dimes
roll through the snack machine.
We pretend that it's a meal
and give thanks and
for even five minutes
we can talk ourselves into being
gathered at home.

But in the end, we leave in darkness
exiting through the same gray lobby
into the quickening night.

Every one of us leaves a piece
of ourselves behind.
Something, perhaps, as intangible
as the reflection of a face
inside the cold panes of glass
surrounding the lobby door.

FINALE

They are alone.
No one exits or enters,
no sound of hushed voices
from beyond the door,
no hum of machines,
no schedule of medications.
The bustle of the dying has faded
into the quiet of the room.
Even the click and whir of the fan
is silent. No one knows when
the quiet started or when it will end.

What are these pieces of a life
that remain? Tiny treasures
sitting on glass shelves.
Bric-a-brac story tellers,
each one a different chapter.
Who will tell their stories now
that the voice of the room is gone?

In this new silence, dust begins to settle
again – in corners, over mirrors,
and back on the glass shelves.
A lone cobweb leans over the side
beckoning the inhabitants below
to climb up its fragile stairs.

Dust also settles over the living,
bringing tears to their eyes,
sticking in their throats.
Cobwebs lacing memories to each other.

At the end of the day, it is the quiet
comfort of the dust that settles us.
A visible reminder of what is to come.

The Return

~ Greatness lives in one who triumphs equally over defeat and victory

(Steinbeck, *The Acts of King Arthur and His Noble Knights*)

SNOW WHITE'S MATH PROBLEM

If seven dwarves each own
seven shirts, seven pairs of socks,
seven pairs of pants, and
seven pairs of boxers,
then how much money does
Snow White have to pay
for laundry, so she
can hang out in the forest
with friends, smoking
and reading cheap magazines?

Evva

for Andi's grandma

On the day Grandma put
her purse inside the clothes dryer
Greg came home from work early.
We sat on the back porch
eating home-made root beer floats.
Life was good.

The week the neighbors washed
Grandma's front-room curtains
we were out of town.
We sat on the boat dock
eating fish sandwiches with fries.
Life was simple.

In the moment Grandma insisted
an intruder had stolen
a six-inch length of sheer curtain,
we stood in the window box
looking at the neat curtain hems.
Life was confusing.

Before we could stop her, Grandma
called the police to report
the missing piece of curtains
and the possible theft of short sheerness
filming her view to the outside world.
We sat around the kitchen table

sipping coffee from chipped mugs
listening as she spoke with the deputy
who patiently waited for her to finish.
Life seemed short.

When the deputy questioned Grandma
about the theft of curtain bottoms,
the strange way the thief had hemmed
the remnants he left behind,
when he asked about other missing items
we all watched Grandma take
her purse out of the dryer
check on her wallet, cash, cards.
Later, we offered the deputy pie and coffee,
which we ate in silence in the front room,
watching the curtains blow in the afternoon breeze.
Life was mysterious and life-like and it was good.

RAGE POEM

Sometimes rage is all we have
says the poet introducing his work,
and I realize that rage kept me alive
those years when nothing else mattered.

Rage was the dark tunnel
I could not put words to.

Rage was the electricity
moving my legs and hands.

Rage fueled the memory of my lungs
so I would not forget to breathe.

I suppose I have never properly thanked Rage,
nor, for that matter, its sponsors
who threw me into that abyss.
The ones who abandoned me
and now envy my wonderful life.

THE THREE LITTLE PIGS

Their three bedroom brick colonial
sold for above-market value
to a family who wanted a big yard
on the outskirts of the city.

The bachelor-brothers moved
to a condo close to downtown,
where they did not have to fear
the sound of the wind at their door.

They pursued hobbies
like building dollhouses
with furniture made of toothpicks,
reading architecture magazines.

Mostly, the pigs loved the safety
of being sandwiched between
the apartments on either side
and the pink orange purple
of sunset on the balcony.

They only lay awake at night
when one of them found
a clump of black fur
stuck in the iron curtains
of the fireplace doors.

The Painted Lady

(for the Haitian earthquake victims)

I.

The wind whispers no warning,
spirits within are unaware as they rouse
in restless insomnia,
Ancestors have no sign to give.
The Painted Lady is coming
to bring the taste of dust to our lips.

The aftershocks of all our losses
reverberate, tremble through us and
we are brought to our knees
with dust, earth, rubble.

Dust and ancestors and bones and dust and pain and desire
and dust and freedom and dust and slavery and dust.

Suffocating dust of dream-like ghosts
freed from earth when rumbling begins.
Tectonic shifts and plates grinding
bones of dead ancestors.

The Painted Lady has come,
walks among us
living and dead and dust.

II.

Dust settles among us, in every crevice
snows upon the city
quiets crash of walls
muffles cries, sobs of injured.
Dust coats lost darkness survivors,
accented by boom of exploding electrical boxes.

While chasms shift below,
Silent dust permeates every space,
talcum fine baby powder dust,
coating the cilia of hairs in nose and lungs
rising in a cloud like the second coming.

See the woman in the distance,
painted like a tribal dancer?
Dust and blood thicken upon her.
The Painted Lady is here.

III.

She stands and absorbs the dust,
blood, rubble, bodies.
Spirits of earth and rock
of ancestors and trees wander
confused by her presence.
Why has she called them forth with no warning,
what does she want with her dust and destruction?
Soon the tears will flow, leaving tracks,
and bringing rain to the living,
thickening the dust to mud
while the Painted Lady watches.

IV.

Mud and dust.
Dust and mud.
Mud born of disaster, like their cousin Katrina,
mud born of poverty,
mud under the nail of the oppressor's thumb.
Mud of despair, of hopelessness
mud in your pores, in your blood.

Mud and dust and
corpses piling in roadways mud,
families vanished dust,
collapsed buildings mud,
infected drinking water mud/dust,
hunger dust,
back alley amputations mud/blood,
sleeping on streets dust,
tears and anguish mud,
muffled cries of despair dust.

Dust and mud settling
before the last tremors
destroy the hopes of the living.

V.

Before she vanishes into the confusion,
the Painted Lady opens her lips
to blow dust one last time
leave us with the taste of her kiss.
Dust settles over the words

barely formed in our mouths
Yéle Haiti. Freedom will be ours.

Elegy for RCG

after Naomi Shihab Nye

We are looking for your laugh
your smile with crinkled eyes
looking for a way back to it
through faded lavender.
Listening for your chime
in the wind,
hint of soprano bells,
feeling your touch
at the piano,
eyes half-closed
finger raised to keep time.
We see your ardent smile
at both sides of a day.
How was it, you lived
in everything we did,
all the music sung, strings
humming sorrows and victory,
amongst the chaos you both hated
and loved in us, all the dust
from our lives intersecting?
We look for you now in the notes
of a song we have written together
but forgot the words.
Your music poured into us
and those who come after,
seeds carried on the wind
chimes under the pecan trees.

A Day in the Life

He could be a typical boy
of twelve or thirteen,
wearing jeans,
a baggy t-shirt,
sneakers whose laces
are too long.

He probably likes
to play soccer,
hang with his friends,
think about girls.

He could be a typical boy,
but this is Juarez–
a city at war with itself –
there are no typical boys here.

He should study algebra,
chemistry, Mexican history.
Instead, every day is a study
in the poetry of grief.

He might be the boy who
comes home from school
to find his favorite
uncle's head planted
on a stake in the yard,
the body of a brother

bloodied, bruised
just across the threshold.

Every day here is the day of the dead
shrines and altars replaced with chalk outlines,
decapitated bodies left in place
where the last breath had fled.

Is there a name for this kind of survival?
A name for the children who no longer sleep
too afraid of the nightmares?
For the "lucky" ones who cross borders
seeking a safe haven?

A name for the trauma that never goes away
even as the blood fades
from the floor of memory,
even in this new house where
bienvenidos is more than a word
and where there is never time enough to forget.

REPRISE

Even through the dust, we try to parse
this story of a life, these bits on shelves.
Souvenirs from the journey.
And what is life but a journey?
Some say that it's about the trip, not
the destination. What of those left behind
straddling the road?

Our journey is more labyrinth than road.
A tangled maze we navigate blindly.
Here and there we find the string
of a familiar cobweb and we place
a souvenir to remember,
a mark in the dust.

The souvenirs of a lost life sit in this dust.
Each waits to become a marker,
in a new place,
apart from one another,
where the tangle of one maze
intersects the path of another.
Here they will still be the watchers,
connected by a film of cobwebs,
no longer guardians of the path.

GRATITUDE

It is nearly impossible to give thanks to all the people who made this book possible, but I will try.

Special thanks to my sister, Elizabeth "Skeeter" Scheid who provided her amazing watercolor paintings for this book and encouraged me in a way that only a sister can. Thanks to Dave and Steve Scheid who graciously allowed me to use their pictures on the cover. To Vince Scheid, just because. To Joseph Ross who provided assistance with the overall concept of this book. To Moira Dougherty who helped with fairy tale advice and years of faithful friendship. To Dick Norman for patience, friendship, and support. To Michael Gushue for mentoring and guidance. To my friends Sarah Browning, Larry Joseph, Andi Kotch, Laura Marks, Peter Montgomery, Melissa Tuckey, Dan Vera, and the writers on Three Elements and Thirty Poems blog who provided invaluable comments on these poems. To everyone I ever begged to read my work, thanks for all the years of encouragement, I could not have accomplished this without you. To my parents, Ruth and George Scheid, who instilled a love of all things written and poetic and who encouraged my artistic endeavors. To Aunt B who was a role model for a creative life. Finally, thanks to my own family: Alex and Sam Girardot, for always being my muses, my audience, my critics; and to my husband, Chris Girardot for everything.

Made in the USA
Lexington, KY
17 April 2014